Motivation

Unleash Your Inner Drive and Achieve Your Goals with the
Ultimate Guide to Lasting Motivation: Your Blueprint for a
Fulfilling Life

Lance P. Richards

Motivation: Unleash Your Inner Drive and Achieve Your Goals with the Ultimate Guide to Lasting Motivation: Your Blueprint for a Fulfilling Life

Table of Contents

01: Introduction: Understanding Motivation

Motivation is the driving force behind our actions and the key to achieving our goals. Without motivation, we lack the energy, enthusiasm, and determination to pursue our dreams and live a fulfilling life. So, what exactly is motivation and where does it come from?

Motivation can be defined as the inner drive that compels us to act and pursue our goals. It is the spark that ignites our ambition and fuels our passion. Motivation comes in many forms, such as the desire to achieve success, to make a positive impact in the world, to overcome challenges, to learn and grow, or to find happiness and fulfillment.

However, motivation can also be elusive and unpredictable. One day, you may feel highly motivated and eager to tackle your goals, while the next day, you may feel discouraged and lacking in energy. This is because motivation is not a constant state, but a dynamic and ever-changing process.

So, how can we tap into our inner drive and maintain a high level of motivation? The answer lies in understanding the science of motivation and the various factors that influence it.

One of the key factors is our mindset. Our mindset refers to the way we think about ourselves, our abilities, and our potential. If we have a growth mindset, we believe in our ability to grow and improve, and we embrace challenges as opportunities to learn and develop. On the other hand, if we have a fixed mindset, we believe that our abilities are set and unchangeable, and we may avoid challenges and give up easily.

Another important factor is our emotions. Our emotions play a crucial role in our motivation, as they can either boost or undermine our drive. Positive emotions, such as happiness, excitement, and satisfaction, can energize us and inspire us to pursue our goals. Negative emotions, such as fear, frustration, and stress, can drain us and cause us to lose motivation.

Furthermore, our environment and the people around us can greatly impact our motivation. A supportive and encouraging environment, as well as positive relationships, can boost our confidence and provide us with the encouragement and inspiration we need to stay motivated. On the other hand, a toxic or negative environment, as well as negative relationships, can demoralize us and make it difficult for us to maintain our motivation.

In order to unleash your inner drive and achieve your goals, it is important to understand these factors and how they impact your motivation. By developing a growth mindset, managing your emotions, and creating a supportive environment, you can cultivate lasting motivation and build a fulfilling life.

In this book, we will dive deeper into the science of motivation and explore practical strategies for unlocking your inner drive and achieving your goals. With this ultimate guide to lasting motivation, you will have the tools and the blueprint you need to live a life of purpose, passion, and fulfillment.

02: The Science of Motivation: How Your Brain Works

Have you ever wondered why some days you feel highly motivated and energetic, while other days you struggle to find the motivation to even get out of bed? The answer lies in the science of motivation, specifically how your brain works and the key factors that influence it.

At the core of motivation is the release of neurotransmitters and hormones, such as dopamine and adrenaline, which activate the reward centers in your brain and produce feelings of pleasure and excitement. These neurotransmitters and hormones are triggered by a variety of factors, such as your thoughts, emotions, and experiences.

One of the key drivers of motivation is the concept of goal setting. When you set a goal, your brain creates a neural pathway that is dedicated to pursuing that goal. This pathway activates the release of neurotransmitters and hormones, providing you with the energy and drive you need to achieve your goal.

However, not all goals are created equal. The more challenging and meaningful a goal is, the more neurotransmitters and hormones are released, and the greater the motivation you will experience. On the other hand, if your goal is too easy or unimportant, your brain may not release enough neurotransmitters and hormones to provide you with sufficient motivation.

Another key factor is the level of intrinsic and extrinsic motivation you experience. Intrinsic motivation refers to the drive you feel to pursue a goal because it is inherently fulfilling and meaningful to you. Extrinsic motivation refers to the drive you feel to pursue a goal because of external rewards or punishments, such as money, recognition, or consequences. Research has shown that intrinsic motivation is more powerful and sustainable than extrinsic motivation, as it is less likely to fluctuate and more likely to drive you to persist in the face of challenges.

Moreover, your emotions can greatly impact your motivation. Positive emotions, such as happiness, excitement, and satisfaction, can boost your drive and provide you with the energy and enthusiasm you need to achieve your goals. Negative emotions, such as fear, frustration, and stress, can undermine your motivation and make it difficult for you to focus and perform at your best.

Finally, your environment and the people around you can also play a crucial role in your motivation. A supportive and encouraging environment, as well as positive relationships, can provide you with the encouragement and inspiration you need to stay motivated. On the other hand, a toxic or negative environment, as well as negative relationships, can demoralize you and make it difficult for you to maintain your motivation.

In order to fully unleash your inner drive and achieve your goals, it is important to understand the science of motivation and how your brain works. By setting challenging and meaningful goals, tapping into intrinsic motivation, managing your emotions, and creating a supportive environment, you can tap into the power of your brain and cultivate lasting motivation.

In the following chapters, we will delve deeper into these key factors and explore practical strategies for optimizing your brain and unlocking your inner drive. With this ultimate guide to lasting motivation, you will have the tools and the blueprint you need to unleash your potential and achieve your goals.

03: The Power of Positive Thinking: Overcoming Negative Thoughts

One of the greatest obstacles to motivation is the presence of negative thoughts. These thoughts can sap your energy, undermine your confidence, and make it difficult for you to pursue your goals with the drive and determination you need to succeed.

Negative thoughts can take many forms, such as self-doubt, self-criticism, and negative self-talk. These thoughts can originate from a variety of sources, such as past experiences, societal expectations, and personal insecurities. Whatever their source, negative thoughts can be incredibly powerful and difficult to shake.

However, the good news is that you have the power to overcome negative thoughts and cultivate a positive mindset. Positive thinking is a powerful tool that can help you tap into your motivation and achieve your goals with confidence and clarity.

One of the key strategies for positive thinking is to engage in regular self-reflection and self-awareness. By taking the time to reflect on your thoughts and emotions, you can gain insight into the underlying sources of your negative thoughts and develop strategies for combating them. This might involve challenging negative self-talk with positive affirmations, seeking out supportive relationships, or engaging in self-care practices that promote well-being and resilience.

Another important strategy is to cultivate gratitude and appreciation. By focusing on the things you have to be thankful for, you can shift your perspective and cultivate a more positive outlook. This might involve keeping a gratitude journal, practicing mindfulness, or simply taking the time to appreciate the simple pleasures of life.

It is also important to focus on your strengths and accomplishments, rather than your weaknesses and failures. This might involve setting achievable goals, recognizing and celebrating your successes, and engaging in positive self-talk that reinforces your confidence and self-esteem.

Moreover, it is essential to surround yourself with positive and supportive people. The people you surround yourself with have a huge impact on your thoughts, emotions, and motivation. By seeking out relationships with individuals who are supportive, encouraging, and uplifting, you can create a positive and motivating environment that will help you achieve your goals.

In addition, engaging in physical activity and exercise can also be a powerful tool for promoting positive thinking. Exercise releases endorphins, which are natural mood-boosters that can improve your outlook and help you feel more motivated and energized.

Finally, it is important to embrace challenges and failures as opportunities for growth and learning. Instead of viewing failures as setbacks or as evidence of your lack of worth, view them as opportunities to learn and grow. By embracing challenges and failures with a positive and resilient mindset, you can build your confidence and motivation and unleash your inner drive.

In conclusion, the power of positive thinking is immense and can be a powerful tool for overcoming negative thoughts and tapping into your motivation. By engaging in self-reflection and self-awareness, cultivating gratitude and appreciation, focusing on your strengths and accomplishments, surrounding yourself with positive and supportive people, engaging in physical activity and exercise, and embracing challenges and failures, you can cultivate a positive mindset and unleash your inner drive.

04: The Importance of Self-Awareness: Understanding Your Own Motivation

Self-awareness is a critical component of motivation. Without self-awareness, it is difficult to understand what drives you, what motivates you, and what obstacles may be preventing you from pursuing your goals with the drive and determination you need to succeed.

Self-awareness involves understanding your own thoughts, emotions, values, and motivations. It involves taking the time to reflect on your experiences, your attitudes and beliefs, and your patterns of behavior. By gaining insight into these factors, you can develop a deeper understanding of what motivates you and what may be preventing you from reaching your goals.

One of the key strategies for developing self-awareness is to engage in regular self-reflection and introspection. This might involve journaling, meditating, or simply taking the time to reflect on your thoughts and emotions. By taking the time to reflect on your experiences, you can gain a better understanding of your motivations and what may be preventing you from reaching your goals.

Another important strategy is to seek feedback from others. By seeking out the perspectives of others, you can gain a broader and more accurate understanding of your own motivations and patterns of behavior. This might involve seeking feedback from friends, family, or colleagues, or working with a coach or mentor who can help you develop self-awareness and reach your goals.

It is also important to understand your own values and beliefs. Your values and beliefs are deeply ingrained and shape your perceptions, attitudes, and behaviors. By gaining insight into your values and beliefs, you can better understand your motivations and what drives you. This might involve engaging in activities like taking a personality test or participating in a workshop that focuses on self-awareness and personal growth.

Additionally, it is important to understand your own emotional state and how it impacts your motivation. Emotions play a powerful role in shaping our thoughts and behaviors, and by gaining insight into your emotional state, you can better understand your motivations and what may be preventing you from reaching your goals. This might involve seeking out therapy or counseling, practicing mindfulness or meditation, or engaging in activities that promote emotional regulation and self-care.

Finally, it is important to set achievable and meaningful goals. Goals provide a sense of purpose and direction and can be a powerful motivator. However, it is important to ensure that your goals are aligned with your values, beliefs, and motivations. By setting achievable and meaningful goals, you can tap into your motivation and reach your full potential.

In conclusion, self-awareness is a critical component of motivation. By engaging in self-reflection and introspection, seeking feedback from others, understanding your own values and beliefs, understanding your own emotional state, and setting achievable and meaningful goals, you can develop a deeper understanding of your own motivations and unleash your inner drive.

05: The Benefits of Setting Goals: Why Having a Destination Matters

Goal setting is a critical component of motivation. Having a clear sense of direction and a specific destination in mind can help you focus your efforts, prioritize your time, and achieve your aspirations.

One of the key benefits of goal setting is that it provides structure and direction to your efforts. Without a clear goal in mind, it can be difficult to determine what steps you should take and in what order. Having a specific goal in mind helps you focus your efforts and prioritize your time, enabling you to work towards your desired outcome with greater efficiency and effectiveness.

Goal setting also provides a sense of purpose and direction. When you have a clear destination in mind, it becomes easier to stay motivated and focused on your efforts, even when the going gets tough. Having a goal provides a sense of purpose and helps you see the value and significance of your efforts, even when the journey is long and challenging.

Another key benefit of goal setting is that it enables you to measure your progress and see the results of your efforts. When you have a specific goal in mind, you can track your progress and see the tangible results of your efforts. This can help you stay motivated and focused, as you see the progress you are making towards your desired outcome.

Goal setting also helps you build resilience and determination. Pursuing a goal can be challenging and require hard work and perseverance. But, by setting and working towards specific goals, you can develop the skills and mindset necessary to persist in the face of obstacles and challenges. Over time, this can help you build resilience, determination, and grit, enabling you to achieve greater success in all areas of your life.

Additionally, goal setting can help you develop a growth mindset. When you have a specific goal in mind, you are forced to step outside your comfort zone and challenge yourself. This can help you develop new skills and perspectives, and grow both personally and professionally. Over time, this can help you build a growth mindset, enabling you to tackle new challenges and opportunities with greater confidence and skill.

05: THE BENEFITS OF SETTING GOALS: WHY HAVING A DESTINATION MATTERS

Finally, goal setting provides a sense of accomplishment and satisfaction. When you set and achieve a goal, you feel a sense of pride and satisfaction in your efforts. This can help you build confidence, increase your self-esteem, and boost your motivation to set and achieve even greater goals in the future.

In conclusion, goal setting is a critical component of motivation. By setting specific, measurable, and achievable goals, you can focus your efforts, prioritize your time, and achieve your desired outcomes with greater efficiency and effectiveness. Whether you are seeking to advance your career, improve your health, or achieve a personal dream, goal setting can help you get there. So, unleash your inner drive, set your goals, and take the first step towards a fulfilling and meaningful life.

06: Finding Your Passion: The Key to Lasting Motivation

Have you ever wondered what it would be like to wake up every day with a sense of purpose and excitement about the work you do? To be fully engaged in what you are doing, to feel a deep sense of meaning and satisfaction in your life? The answer to this question is simple: finding your passion.

Your passion is the driving force behind your motivation, the thing that fuels your inner fire and inspires you to take action towards your goals. When you are passionate about something, you are naturally driven to pursue it with energy and enthusiasm, regardless of the challenges you may face.

But how do you find your passion? The truth is, finding your passion can be a journey, and it may take time and effort to uncover what truly inspires you. But, by taking a few key steps, you can tap into your inner drive and discover what truly motivates you.

The first step in finding your passion is to reflect on your interests and strengths. What are you naturally good at? What activities do you enjoy doing in your free time? What topics or subjects do you find yourself consistently drawn to?

06: FINDING YOUR PASSION: THE KEY TO LASTING MOTIVATION

These are all signs of your innate passions and interests, and can help you identify what you are truly passionate about.

Next, explore new interests and experiences. Don't be afraid to try new things and step outside your comfort zone. This can help you expand your horizons and discover new passions and interests that you may not have considered before.

Another key component of finding your passion is to connect with like-minded people. Surrounding yourself with others who share your interests and passions can help you feel inspired and motivated.

07: The Art of Visualization: Bringing Your Goals to Life

Have you ever heard the saying, "What you see is what you get"? Well, this phrase holds true when it comes to visualization. Visualization is the practice of creating a mental image of your goals and desires in your mind's eye. When you visualize, you bring your goals to life and activate your mind's natural ability to make your desires a reality.

Visualization is a powerful tool for motivation because it helps you see your future self already living your goals. This mental image can serve as a source of inspiration and drive, and it can also help you overcome obstacles and negative thoughts. When you visualize, you train your brain to see your future self as someone who has already achieved their goals, and this can help you feel more confident and motivated to take action.

To start visualizing your goals, you need to first define what you want to achieve. Write down your goals in detail, including what you want to accomplish, when you want to achieve it, and why it is important to you. Then, close your eyes and imagine yourself living your goals. See yourself taking action and achieving your goals, and feel the emo-

tions of pride, joy, and accomplishment. Make your visualization as vivid as possible, using all of your senses to create
a real-life mental movie.

It is important to practice visualization regularly, as this
helps to strengthen your connection to your goals and rein-
force your motivation. You can visualize your goals in the
morning and at night, or whenever you feel like you need a
boost of motivation.

In addition to visualization, it can also be helpful to use
visual aids such as vision boards or images that represent
your goals. Seeing your goals in a physical form can help
you stay focused and motivated, and it can also serve as a
reminder of what you are working towards.

Visualization is not just a tool for motivation, but it is also a
tool for manifestation. When you visualize, you send a
powerful message to your subconscious mind that you are
committed to achieving your goals, and this can help you at-
tract the resources and opportunities you need to make
them a reality. So start practicing the art of visualization
today, and watch as your goals come to life.

08: Staying Focused: Avoiding Distractions and Staying on Track

Staying focused is a crucial part of achieving your goals and maintaining motivation. Distractions come in all shapes and sizes, and they can quickly derail your progress and leave you feeling demotivated. To stay focused, it's important to identify and eliminate distractions, set boundaries, and develop strong self-discipline.

One of the biggest distractions in our modern world is technology. From social media to emails to video games, it's easy to get lost in the virtual world and forget about your real-life goals. To avoid these distractions, it's important to set boundaries and limit your screen time. Try turning off your phone during work hours, setting aside time each day for uninterrupted focus, or taking regular breaks from technology.

Another common distraction is procrastination. Procrastination is a habit that can be hard to break, but it's important to understand that it's not a time management issue; it's a motivation issue. To avoid procrastination, it's helpful to break down your goals into smaller, more manageable tasks and prioritize them based on their importance and urgency.

08: STAYING FOCUSED: AVOIDING DISTRACTIONS AND STAYING ON TRACK

You can also create a schedule or to-do list, set deadlines, and hold yourself accountable.

Negative self-talk can also be a major distraction, leading you to doubt your abilities and question your motivation. To overcome negative thoughts, it's important to practice positive self-talk and cultivate a growth mindset. Surround yourself with positive people, read positive affirmations, and focus on your strengths and accomplishments. Remember, the voice in your head can either be your biggest cheerleader or your harshest critic, so choose your thoughts wisely.

Lastly, it's important to understand that distractions will happen, but it's how you respond to them that will determine your success. When you are faced with a distraction, take a step back, refocus, and remind yourself of your goals. Avoid getting discouraged or giving up, and instead use each distraction as an opportunity to grow and learn.

In conclusion, staying focused is essential for lasting motivation and achieving your goals. By identifying and eliminating distractions, setting boundaries, and developing strong self-discipline, you can stay focused and motivated on your path to success. Remember, the journey to your goals is not always easy, but with persistence and dedication, you can overcome any obstacle and reach your destination.

09: Overcoming Procrastination: Taking Action and Achieving Your Dreams

Procrastination is a common challenge that many people face when trying to achieve their goals. It's the habit of putting off tasks and avoiding responsibility, leading to missed opportunities and unfulfilled dreams. While it can be tempting to put things off, procrastination only leads to added stress and decreased motivation. To overcome procrastination and achieve your goals, it's important to understand the root causes and develop strategies to take action.

One of the main reasons people procrastinate is because they lack clarity and direction. When you don't know what you want or how to achieve it, it can be difficult to stay motivated and focused. To overcome this, it's important to set clear and specific goals, create a plan of action, and hold yourself accountable. Write down your goals, break them down into smaller tasks, and schedule time to work on them each day.

Another common cause of procrastination is fear of failure. People may avoid taking action because they are afraid of not succeeding or making mistakes. To overcome this, focus on progress instead of perfection. Embrace mistakes as opportunities for growth and learning, and remember that success is a journey, not a destination. Celebrate your successes, no matter how small, and keep moving forward.

Another factor that contributes to procrastination is boredom or lack of interest. When you don't find a task engaging or meaningful, it's easy to put it off. To overcome this, try to find ways to make the task more interesting, or think about how it fits into your bigger picture and helps you achieve your goals. Surround yourself with supportive and motivated people who share your goals and can help keep you on track.

Finally, distractions can also be a major obstacle to taking action. From social media to emails to household chores, there are many distractions that can pull us away from our goals. To overcome this, create a dedicated workspace, turn off notifications, and minimize distractions. Focus on your tasks and keep your eye on the prize.

In conclusion, procrastination is a common challenge that can be overcome with the right mindset and strategies. By setting clear and specific goals, embracing progress over perfection, making tasks more interesting, and minimizing distractions, you can take action and achieve your dreams. Remember that success is a journey, and that every step forward is a step closer to realizing your goals.

10: Building Confidence: Gaining the Self-Assurance You Need to Succeed

Confidence is a critical component of success. When you believe in yourself and your abilities, you are more likely to take risks and pursue your goals with determination. However, building confidence is not always easy, especially if you have experienced failure or negative self-talk in the past. The good news is that confidence can be developed and strengthened through practice and intentional effort.

One of the key ways to build confidence is to focus on your strengths and accomplishments. Make a list of your achievements and take time to reflect on what you are proud of. Recognize and celebrate your successes, no matter how small, and remind yourself of your worth and abilities. Surround yourself with supportive and encouraging people who believe in you, and avoid those who bring you down.

Another important factor in building confidence is to set realistic and achievable goals. When you accomplish your goals, no matter how small, you build self-efficacy, which is the belief that you can achieve what you set out to do. Start with small and manageable tasks and gradually work your way up to bigger challenges. Celebrate your successes along the way and acknowledge the effort and progress you have made.

It's also important to have a growth mindset, which means embracing challenges and viewing them as opportunities for growth and learning. Instead of focusing on failure, focus on the journey and what you can learn from the experience. Embrace mistakes and setbacks as part of the process, and be open to feedback and constructive criticism.

Confidence can also be strengthened through positive self-talk. Challenge negative thoughts and beliefs, and focus on what you can do, rather than what you can't. Surround yourself with positive affirmations and reminders of your worth, and speak kindly and positively to yourself. Practice gratitude and focus on what you have, rather than what you lack.

Finally, it's important to take care of yourself and prioritize self-care. This means eating well, exercising, getting enough sleep, and engaging in activities that bring you joy and relaxation. When you feel good about yourself, you are more

10: BUILDING CONFIDENCE: GAINING THE SELF-AS-SURANCE YOU NEED TO SUCCEED

likely to believe in yourself and your abilities.

In conclusion, building confidence is a critical component of success, and it takes intentional effort and practice. Focus on your strengths and accomplishments, set realistic and achievable goals, embrace challenges and feedback, engage in positive self-talk, and prioritize self-care. By doing these things, you can build the confidence you need to unleash your inner drive and achieve your goals.

11: Harnessing the Power of Positive Habits: Establishing Healthy Routines

In this chapter, we will delve into the importance of establishing positive habits in order to achieve our goals and maintain motivation. Habits are powerful things - they can either help us or hinder us in our pursuit of success and fulfillment. By developing healthy routines and repeating them consistently, we can create an environment that supports our motivation and drives us towards our goals.

One of the key benefits of positive habits is that they can help us develop a sense of control over our lives. When we establish routines, we are taking charge of our time and our activities, which can help us feel more in control and confident in our ability to achieve our goals.

Another important aspect of positive habits is that they can help us create momentum. When we develop a habit of doing something, it becomes easier to continue doing it over time. This is because we have established a routine, and our brain has learned to associate that behavior with a specific time or place. As a result, we are less likely to forget to do it, and we are more likely to do it automatically.

However, developing positive habits is not always easy. It can be difficult to establish new routines, especially if they are different from our current habits. To help you in this process, it is important to have a clear understanding of why you want to establish a new habit. This will help you stay motivated and focused, even when the going gets tough.

Another important step in developing positive habits is to make them achievable and realistic. Start small, and gradually increase the difficulty level as you get more comfortable with the habit. For example, if you want to start exercising every day, you might begin by doing 5 minutes of stretching each morning, and gradually increase the time as you get stronger and more confident.

In addition to setting achievable goals, it is important to also reward yourself for your efforts. Positive reinforcement can be a great motivator, and can help you feel good about your progress and encourage you to continue with your new habit. Whether it's treating yourself to a movie or your favorite meal, or simply taking some time to relax and reflect on your progress, find something that works for you and stick with it.

Finally, it is important to be patient and persistent in your pursuit of positive habits. Developing new routines takes time, and it may take several attempts before you get it right. Don't get discouraged - instead, focus on making small, steady progress and remind yourself of why you wanted to establish the habit in the first place.

In conclusion, positive habits are a powerful tool for achieving your goals and maintaining lasting motivation. By establishing routines, taking control of your time, rewarding yourself for your efforts, and being patient and persistent, you can develop habits that will help you achieve your dreams and live a more fulfilling life.

12: The Importance of Self-Care: Nurturing Your Body and Mind

Self-care is a critical component of maintaining lasting motivation and achieving your goals. Without taking care of yourself, you may find yourself feeling burned out, stressed, and lacking the energy and drive necessary to push forward towards your dreams. In this chapter, we'll explore the importance of self-care and how it can help you unleash your inner drive and achieve your goals.

Self-care can take many different forms, from exercise and healthy eating to hobbies and relaxation. Some examples of self-care activities include:

– Exercise: Regular physical activity has been shown to reduce stress, improve mood, and increase overall energy levels. Whether it's hitting the gym or going for a walk, incorporating exercise into your routine can help you stay motivated and focused on your goals.

– Healthy eating: Eating a well-balanced diet is essential for maintaining good health and energy levels. Filling your body with nutritious foods, such as fruits and vegetables, will provide you with the fuel you need to tackle your goals.

12: THE IMPORTANCE OF SELF-CARE: NURTURING YOUR BODY AND MIND

– Hobbies and interests: Pursuing hobbies and interests that bring you joy and relaxation can help reduce stress and increase overall happiness. Whether it's painting, playing an instrument, or gardening, taking time to engage in activities you enjoy can help keep you motivated and focused on your goals.

– Sleep: Getting adequate sleep is crucial for maintaining good health and overall well-being. Lack of sleep can lead to fatigue, irritability, and decreased motivation, making it more difficult to achieve your goals.

– Mindfulness and meditation: Practicing mindfulness and meditation can help reduce stress, improve focus, and increase self-awareness. By taking time to reflect and focus inward, you can gain a better understanding of your motivations and what drives you towards your goals.

By incorporating self-care into your routine, you can cultivate a healthier, happier, and more motivated mindset, helping you unleash your inner drive and achieve your goals. Whether it's through exercise, healthy eating, hobbies and interests, sleep, or mindfulness and meditation, taking care of yourself is a critical part of maintaining lasting motiva-

12: THE IMPORTANCE OF SELF-CARE: NURTURING YOUR BODY AND MIND

tion and reaching your full potential.

13: The Power of Gratitude: Appreciating What You Have

Gratitude is a powerful tool that can greatly enhance our lives and help us achieve our goals. When we focus on what we have, rather than what we lack, we can feel more satisfied and fulfilled, which can help us maintain a positive outlook even during difficult times. In this chapter, we'll explore the many benefits of gratitude and how it can help us cultivate lasting motivation.

First and foremost, gratitude helps us cultivate a positive mindset. When we focus on what we're grateful for, we tend to think more optimistically, which can help us feel more confident and motivated. Gratitude also helps us develop a more grateful attitude towards life, which can help us appreciate and make the most of each day.

Another benefit of gratitude is that it can help us build and maintain strong relationships. When we express gratitude to others, we strengthen our connections with them and show that we value their contributions. This can help us foster a supportive network of friends, family, and coworkers, which can provide us with the support and encouragement we need to stay motivated and reach our goals.

13: THE POWER OF GRATITUDE: APPRECIATING WHAT YOU HAVE

Gratitude can also help us overcome feelings of jealousy, envy, and resentment. When we focus on what we're grateful for, it can help us shift our focus away from what we don't have and towards what we do have. This can help us feel more content and less likely to compare ourselves to others, which can help us maintain a positive outlook and avoid feeling discouraged.

Finally, gratitude can help us improve our physical and emotional well-being. Studies have shown that people who practice gratitude experience reduced levels of stress and anxiety, improved sleep, and increased feelings of happiness and well-being. Additionally, gratitude can help us develop a more optimistic outlook, which can help us better handle difficult situations and cope with challenges in a healthy way.

In conclusion, the power of gratitude is immense, and it can play a significant role in helping us cultivate lasting motivation. By focusing on what we're grateful for, we can cultivate a positive mindset, build strong relationships, overcome negative emotions, and improve our overall well-being. So, take the time to practice gratitude each day and experience

13: THE POWER OF GRATITUDE: APPRECIATING WHAT YOU HAVE

the many benefits it has to offer.

14: Finding Your Inner Strength: Overcoming Obstacles and Challenges

Introduction:

The journey towards achieving your goals and realizing your full potential can be a long and difficult one. There will be obstacles, challenges, and setbacks along the way that can make it easy to lose motivation and give up. But it is important to remember that you have the inner strength and resilience to overcome these challenges and achieve your goals. In this chapter, we will explore the power of finding your inner strength and how it can help you stay motivated and on track towards realizing your dreams.

What is Inner Strength?

Inner strength refers to the mental and emotional fortitude that allows individuals to endure difficult situations, overcome obstacles, and maintain their focus and motivation. It is a combination of resilience, determination, and confidence that gives individuals the ability to face challenges head-on and overcome them. Inner strength is often developed through life experiences and can be strengthened through intentional practices and self-reflection.

How to Find Your Inner Strength:

– Reflect on Your Past Experiences: Take some time to think about the challenges you have faced in the past and how you overcame them. Reflecting on these experiences can help you build confidence in your abilities and resilience.

– Practice Mindfulness: Mindfulness practices such as meditation and deep breathing can help you become more self-aware and develop a greater sense of inner strength. By paying attention to your thoughts, feelings, and sensations, you can learn to better understand and regulate your emotions.

– Surround Yourself with Positive Influences: Surrounding yourself with positive, supportive individuals can help you build confidence and develop your inner strength. Seek out people who are supportive, encouraging, and help you to see your own potential.

– Focus on Self-Care: Taking care of your physical and mental well-being is crucial for developing inner strength.

14: FINDING YOUR INNER STRENGTH: OVERCOMING OBSTACLES AND CHALLENGES

Regular exercise, a healthy diet, and adequate sleep can all help you feel more confident and resilient.

– Embrace Challenges: Embracing challenges and viewing them as opportunities for growth can help you develop your inner strength. By embracing challenges, you can learn to see setbacks as temporary and grow from them.

– Cultivate a Growth Mindset: Adopting a growth mindset, where you see challenges and setbacks as opportunities for growth, can help you develop your inner strength. By focusing on the process of growth and learning, rather than the outcome, you can better handle setbacks and overcome obstacles.

Conclusion:

Finding your inner strength is a crucial part of staying motivated and achieving your goals. By reflecting on your past experiences, practicing mindfulness, surrounding yourself with positive influences, focusing on self-care, embracing challenges, and cultivating a growth mindset, you can build the mental and emotional fortitude needed to overcome obstacles and achieve your dreams. Remember, the journey towards success and fulfillment can be difficult, but with the right tools and mindset, you have the strength and resilience to overcome any challenge and achieve your goals.

15: Building Resilience: Bouncing Back from Setbacks

Resilience is the ability to overcome adversity, bounce back from setbacks, and keep moving forward in the face of obstacles and challenges. It is a critical component of lasting motivation and can help you stay focused, stay positive, and maintain your drive even when things get tough. Building resilience is not easy, but it is possible with the right mindset, the right tools, and the right approach.

One of the first things you need to do in order to build resilience is to develop a growth mindset. This means embracing challenges as opportunities for growth and learning, instead of fearing them. When you have a growth mindset, you see obstacles as stepping stones, not as roadblocks. You view setbacks as learning experiences, not as reasons to give up. You understand that success is a journey, not a destination, and that setbacks are simply part of the process.

Another key to building resilience is to focus on your strengths and build on them. When you know what you are good at, you can focus your energy and effort on what really matters to you, and you can achieve your goals with more confidence and ease. When you build your strengths, you

44

also build your self-esteem and your sense of self-worth, which are essential for lasting motivation.

In addition to focusing on your strengths, it is also important to cultivate a supportive network of friends, family, and colleagues who will encourage you and help you stay positive and motivated, even when things get tough. This network can provide you with the emotional and psychological support you need to stay motivated and keep moving forward, even when you face challenges and obstacles.

Another important factor in building resilience is to take care of your physical and emotional well-being. This means eating a healthy diet, getting regular exercise, getting enough sleep, and managing stress through mindfulness practices and self-care activities like meditation, yoga, and journaling. When you take care of your physical and emotional well-being, you are better equipped to handle stress and to remain motivated, even in the face of challenges.

Finally, it is important to be intentional about building resilience. This means setting goals, tracking your progress, and taking concrete steps to develop your resilience skills. For example, you might set a goal to practice mindfulness for 10 minutes a day, to exercise for 30 minutes a day, or to practice gratitude by writing down three things you are thankful for each day.

By following these tips, and by being intentional and persistent in your efforts, you can build resilience and develop the inner strength and determination you need to stay motivated and achieve your goals, no matter what obstacles you may face. So go ahead and start building your resilience today, and unleash your inner drive and achieve the life of your dreams.

16: Embracing Change: Adapting to Life's Transitions

Change is a natural part of life and it is inevitable. However, it can be difficult to embrace and adapt to new situations, especially if they come unexpectedly. In order to achieve your goals and maintain lasting motivation, it is important to develop a positive attitude towards change and to be able to adapt to new circumstances with ease.

One of the keys to embracing change is to have an open mind. You need to be willing to consider new possibilities and to see things from a different perspective. It is also important to have a growth mindset, which means that you believe in your ability to learn and grow, even in the face of challenges.

Another way to embrace change is to focus on the opportunities it presents, rather than the challenges. When faced with a new situation, try to see it as an opportunity for growth, learning, and personal development. This positive outlook will help you to be more resilient and better equipped to handle change.

It is also important to develop strong coping skills. This

means learning how to manage your emotions and stress effectively, so that you can remain calm and focused in the face of change. For example, you can practice mindfulness, exercise regularly, or seek support from friends and family.

Finally, it is important to take action when faced with change. Rather than simply feeling overwhelmed or anxious, take steps to move forward and make the most of the situation. This could involve seeking out new opportunities, learning new skills, or seeking support from others.

In conclusion, embracing change is a critical component of lasting motivation. By developing a positive attitude towards change, focusing on the opportunities it presents, developing strong coping skills, and taking action, you can become more resilient and better equipped to handle life's transitions. So, embrace change and let it drive you towards your goals and a fulfilling life!

17: The Benefits of Exercise: Boosting Your Physical and Mental Health

Introduction:

Exercise is a crucial component of a healthy lifestyle, and its benefits extend far beyond just physical health. Regular exercise has been shown to have a positive impact on mental health and motivation, making it an essential part of your journey to unlocking your inner drive and achieving your goals. In this chapter, we'll explore the many benefits of exercise and why it should be an integral part of your routine.

The Physical Benefits of Exercise:

First and foremost, exercise is essential for maintaining physical health. Regular physical activity helps to reduce the risk of numerous diseases, including heart disease, diabetes, and some forms of cancer. Exercise also improves cardiovascular health by strengthening the heart and reducing the risk of stroke and heart attack. Additionally, regular exercise can help you to maintain a healthy weight, reduce your risk of obesity, and improve your overall physical fitness.

17: THE BENEFITS OF EXERCISE: BOOSTING YOUR PHYSICAL AND MENTAL HEALTH

The Mental Benefits of Exercise:

The benefits of exercise don't end with physical health. Regular physical activity has been shown to have a profound impact on mental health, reducing the risk of depression, anxiety, and other mental health conditions. Exercise also helps to reduce stress and increase feelings of well-being and happiness. This is due to the release of endorphins, the "feel-good" hormones, that are produced when you exercise.

Boosting Your Motivation:

One of the most significant benefits of exercise is its impact on motivation. Regular physical activity can help you to feel more energized and motivated to tackle the challenges of daily life. Exercise can also help you to feel more confident and capable, which can have a positive impact on your motivation. Additionally, regular exercise can help you to establish healthy habits, which can further boost your motivation and help you to achieve your goals.

Finding an Exercise Routine that Works for You:

The key to reaping the benefits of exercise is to find a

routine that works for you. Some people enjoy high-intensity workouts, such as running or cycling, while others prefer more low-impact activities, such as yoga or swimming. It's important to choose an exercise routine that you enjoy and that you're able to stick to. This will help you to establish a consistent routine and to see the benefits of exercise over the long term.

Conclusion:

In conclusion, exercise is a critical component of a healthy and motivated lifestyle. Regular physical activity can improve physical health, mental health, and motivation, making it an essential part of your journey to unlocking your inner drive and achieving your goals. So, whether you prefer high-intensity workouts or low-impact activities, make sure to incorporate exercise into your daily routine and experience the many benefits for yourself.

18: The Importance of Sleep: Recharging Your Body and Mind

Chapter Title: The Importance of Sleep: Recharging Your Body and Mind

Sleep is one of the most important aspects of our daily lives, and it plays a vital role in our physical and mental health. The human body needs sleep in order to function at its best, and without it, we can experience a wide range of negative effects, from decreased energy and concentration, to increased stress levels and an increased risk of illness. In this chapter, we will explore the importance of sleep and how it can impact our motivation and overall well-being.

Why Sleep Matters

Sleep is essential for the body to repair and rejuvenate itself, both physically and mentally. During sleep, our bodies are able to heal and regenerate damaged cells, and our brains are able to consolidate new memories and process information from the day. In addition, sleep helps regulate our hormones, including cortisol, the stress hormone, and insulin, which is important for controlling blood sugar levels.

18: THE IMPORTANCE OF SLEEP: RECHARGING YOUR BODY AND MIND

Lack of sleep can have serious consequences on our physical and mental health. When we don't get enough sleep, our bodies can become fatigued and our mental functions can become impaired, making it difficult to concentrate, remember information, and make decisions. Additionally, lack of sleep can increase our risk for developing a number of health problems, including obesity, diabetes, heart disease, and depression.

The Connection Between Sleep and Motivation

Sleep and motivation are deeply connected, as our levels of motivation are directly tied to our energy levels and overall well-being. When we are well-rested, we are more likely to have the energy and focus necessary to pursue our goals, while lack of sleep can leave us feeling sluggish and unmotivated.

One of the biggest benefits of getting enough sleep is that it helps improve our mood and reduce stress levels. When we are sleep deprived, our bodies produce more cortisol, which can increase feelings of anxiety and depression. On the other hand, adequate sleep can help reduce cortisol levels, allowing us to feel more relaxed and positive. This can have a significant impact on our motivation, as it helps us feel better about ourselves and our ability to pursue our goals.

Tips for Better Sleep

If you are struggling with getting enough sleep, there are a number of simple changes you can make to improve the quality of your sleep. Some of these tips include:

– Establishing a consistent sleep routine: Go to bed and wake up at the same time every day, even on weekends. This will help regulate your body's internal clock and make it easier to fall asleep and wake up feeling refreshed.

– Creating a sleep-conducive environment: Keep your sleeping area cool, dark, and quiet, and invest in a comfortable mattress and pillows.

– Avoiding caffeine, alcohol, and nicotine before bedtime: These substances can interfere with your sleep and make it harder to fall asleep.

– Engaging in physical activity: Exercise can help improve the quality of your sleep, but it's important to avoid engaging in strenuous activity close to bedtime, as it can take several hours for your body to calm down.

– Relaxing before bedtime: Engage in activities such as reading, meditation, or yoga to help calm your mind and relax your body.

In conclusion, sleep is a vital component of our overall well-being, and it plays a crucial role in our ability to stay motivated and achieve our goals. By making small changes to our daily routine, we can improve the quality of our sleep and enjoy all the benefits that come with it. Whether it's increased energy, reduced stress, or improved mood, a good night's sleep is essential for unlocking our full potential and living a fulfilling life.

19: Building Strong Relationships: The Power of Social Support

In this chapter, we will delve into the importance of building strong relationships and the power of social support in maintaining lasting motivation. We all need human connection, and research has shown that having a strong support system can improve our mental health and well-being. Whether it's family, friends, or coworkers, our relationships can play a significant role in how we feel about ourselves and our ability to pursue our goals.

One of the key benefits of having strong relationships is that they can provide us with a sense of belonging. When we feel connected to others, we feel less isolated, and we have a greater sense of security. This sense of belonging can increase our self-esteem, which can have a positive impact on our motivation. If we feel good about ourselves, we are more likely to have the confidence to pursue our goals and to persevere when obstacles arise.

Moreover, social support can also help us in our times of need. When we are struggling or going through a difficult time, our friends and family can offer us comfort and encouragement. They can provide a sounding board for our thoughts and feelings, and they can offer us practical support, such as help with tasks or lending an ear when we need to vent. Having people in our lives who are there for us can give us the strength to push through when our motivation starts to wane.

In addition to providing emotional support, our relationships can also play a role in helping us achieve our goals. For example, having a workout buddy can help us stay motivated to exercise regularly. If we have friends or family members who share similar goals, we can work together to achieve them. This not only makes the process more enjoyable, but it can also provide accountability, as we are more likely to stick to our plans if we have others counting on us.

Moreover, relationships can also provide us with new ideas and perspectives. Our friends and family can offer us different viewpoints and provide us with insights that we might not have considered otherwise. This can help us broaden our thinking and find new ways to achieve our goals.

Building strong relationships takes effort, but it is well worth it. When we have people in our lives who care about us, support us, and share our goals, our motivation is more likely to endure. So, take the time to invest in your relationships. Reach out to your friends and family, and make an effort to build new connections. By doing so, you'll be creating a strong support system that will help you stay motivated and achieve your goals.

In conclusion, building strong relationships and having a supportive network of people in our lives is essential for maintaining lasting motivation. Social support can provide us with a sense of belonging, comfort in times of need, accountability, and new ideas and perspectives. So, invest in your relationships and build a strong support system that will help you achieve your goals and live a fulfilling life.

20: The Benefits of Giving: Making a Difference in the World

As human beings, we all have an inherent desire to make a positive impact on the world around us. Whether it's volunteering our time, donating money, or simply lending a listening ear to someone in need, giving can be a powerful source of motivation and fulfillment. In this chapter, we will explore the many benefits of giving and why it should be a central part of our lives.

First and foremost, giving has the power to make a significant impact in the lives of others. Whether we are helping someone in need, supporting a worthy cause, or simply spreading kindness and positivity, the impact of our giving can be immense. By giving to others, we have the opportunity to make a difference in the world and leave a legacy that will endure long after we are gone.

In addition to making a positive impact, giving can also have a profound impact on our own well being. Research has shown that giving can increase our sense of purpose and happiness, boost our self-esteem, and reduce feelings of stress and anxiety. It can also help to build stronger social connections and foster a sense of community.

20: THE BENEFITS OF GIVING: MAKING A DIFFER-
ENCE IN THE WORLD

Another benefit of giving is that it can help us to cultivate a growth mindset. When we give to others, we are demonstrating our willingness to step outside of our comfort zone, take risks, and try new things. This can help us to develop resilience and build the confidence we need to succeed in life.

Giving can also help us to build gratitude and appreciation for the many blessings in our lives. When we take the time to help others and make a difference in their lives, we are reminded of how much we have to be grateful for and how much we have to offer. This can help to shift our focus from what we lack to what we have, and create a more positive outlook on life.

Finally, giving can help us to foster a sense of connection and community. When we work together to help others, we build relationships, develop a sense of belonging, and create a stronger, more supportive community.

In conclusion, giving is a powerful source of motivation and fulfillment that can bring meaning and purpose to our lives. Whether we are helping someone in need, supporting a worthy cause, or simply spreading kindness and positivity,

20: THE BENEFITS OF GIVING: MAKING A DIFFER-ENCE IN THE WORLD

the benefits of giving are many and profound. By incorporating giving into our lives, we can make a positive impact on the world, build stronger relationships, cultivate resilience and gratitude, and find the lasting motivation we need to achieve our goals.

21: The Power of Mindfulness: Living in the Present Moment

Mindfulness is a powerful tool that can help you increase your motivation and live a more fulfilling life. It involves paying attention to your thoughts and experiences in the present moment, without judgment. This practice can help you to reduce stress and anxiety, increase your focus and concentration, and enhance your overall well-being.

Many people believe that mindfulness is a form of meditation. While it can be practiced through meditation, it is also possible to incorporate mindfulness into your daily life through simple, yet intentional, practices. For example, you might try to focus your attention on your breath as you go about your day, or you might try to be fully present in each moment as you interact with others.

One of the key benefits of mindfulness is that it can help you to gain a greater sense of perspective. When you are focused on the present moment, you are less likely to be caught up in worry or anxiety about the future or regret about the past. This can help you to see situations and challenges more objectively, and can give you the clarity you need to make better decisions.

21: THE POWER OF MINDFULNESS: LIVING IN THE PRESENT MOMENT

In addition to increasing your perspective, mindfulness can also help you to cultivate greater self-awareness. When you are mindful, you are more likely to notice your thoughts and feelings as they arise. This can help you to identify patterns of behavior that may be holding you back, and can give you the tools you need to make positive changes.

If you are interested in incorporating mindfulness into your life, there are many resources available to help you get started. There are books, podcasts, and websites that provide information and guidance on mindfulness practices, and there are also many meditation and yoga studios that offer classes and workshops.

It is important to remember that mindfulness is a practice, and that it takes time and dedication to see the benefits. However, with persistence and patience, you will likely find that mindfulness can help you to cultivate greater motivation, and that it can help you to live a more fulfilling life.

To get started with mindfulness, try to set aside a few minutes each day to focus your attention on your breath. You might also try to be more intentional in your interactions with others, and to pay close attention to your thoughts and feelings as they arise. With time and practice, you will likely find that mindfulness becomes a natural and integral part of your daily routine.

22: The Benefits of Reading: Expanding Your Mind and Inspiring Your Dreams

Reading is a powerful tool that can greatly enhance your motivation and help you achieve your goals. By exposing you to new ideas, perspectives, and information, reading can broaden your horizons and inspire you to pursue your passions. It can also help you gain new insights and skills, which can increase your confidence and drive.

One of the benefits of reading is that it provides a source of inspiration. Whether you're reading a novel, a self-help book, or a biography, you can find inspiration from the stories, experiences, and wisdom of others. Reading can help you see the world in a new light and show you what is possible. It can also help you find your own inner motivation and give you the courage to pursue your dreams.

Reading can also be a form of escapism. When you're feeling overwhelmed or stressed, immersing yourself in a good book can help you escape reality and recharge your batteries. Whether you're reading a fantasy novel, a mystery, or a romance, you can get lost in the story and forget about your problems for a while. This can be especially helpful when you're struggling to find motivation or need a break from the pressures of daily life.

In addition to providing inspiration and escapism, reading can also improve your cognitive abilities. By exposing you to new information and challenging your brain to process it, reading can help you build your knowledge, increase your vocabulary, and enhance your problem-solving skills. This can be especially helpful if you're looking to advance your career or improve your personal and professional life.

Reading can also have a positive impact on your mental health. By providing a source of comfort and distraction, reading can help reduce stress and anxiety. It can also provide a sense of calm and relaxation, helping you unwind and recharge after a long day. Reading can also help you process your emotions and provide a space for introspection and self-reflection.

However, reading is not just about the benefits it provides. It's also about the joy and satisfaction of the experience itself. Whether you're reading for personal growth, entertainment, or to gain new knowledge, reading is a rewarding activity that can bring you happiness and fulfillment. It's a great way to spend your free time and can be a source of comfort and joy for years to come.

In conclusion, the benefits of reading are numerous and far-reaching. By inspiring you, providing escapism, improving your cognitive abilities, and having a positive impact on your mental health, reading can be a valuable tool in your journey towards lasting motivation and success. So, find a book that speaks to you, get comfortable, and start exploring the world of literature today!

23: The Importance of Learning: Keeping Your Mind Active and Engaged

Introduction

Learning is one of the most important aspects of personal growth and development. Whether you are trying to improve your professional skills, expand your knowledge in a specific area, or simply stay curious and engaged, ongoing learning is essential. However, with so many distractions and competing priorities in our daily lives, it can be difficult to prioritize and make time for learning. In this chapter, we will explore the many benefits of learning and provide practical tips and strategies to help you make the most of this essential activity.

The Benefits of Learning

– Improves Mental Acuity: Learning new information and skills helps to keep your brain active and engaged, which can improve cognitive function and delay the onset of age-related decline.

– Increases Self-Confidence: As you gain knowledge and

skills in a particular area, you become more confident in your abilities and better equipped to handle challenges.

– Provides a Sense of Accomplishment: Learning something new can be rewarding and provide a sense of accomplishment, which can increase motivation and boost self-esteem.

– Expands Career Opportunities: By developing new skills and knowledge, you increase your marketability and may open up new career opportunities.

– Enhances Problem-Solving Abilities: As you gain knowledge in a specific area, you become better equipped to analyze and solve problems, which can be valuable in both personal and professional contexts.

– Increases Adaptability: In today's rapidly changing world, it is essential to be able to adapt and adjust to new situations and technologies. Ongoing learning helps to keep you up-to-date and adaptable in the face of change.

Tips for Making the Most of Your Learning

– Set Specific Goals: Start by setting clear and specific learning goals for yourself. This could be something as simple as reading a certain number of books in a particular subject or taking a course to develop a new skill.

– Create a Learning Plan: Once you have established your learning goals, create a plan to help you achieve them. This may include setting aside specific times each week for learning, finding resources or classes to support your goals, and breaking larger goals into smaller, more manageable steps.

– Make Learning a Priority: In order to make the most of your learning, it is essential to prioritize this activity. This may mean rearranging your schedule or saying no to other commitments in order to make time for learning.

– Find a Learning Community: Participating in a learning community, such as a book club, study group, or online forum, can help keep you motivated and provide valuable support and insights.

– Incorporate Learning into Daily Life: Make learning a part of your daily routine by finding ways to integrate it into your daily activities. This could include listening to educational podcasts or audiobooks during your commute, or reading articles or books on subjects of interest during your lunch break.

– Stay Motivated: Finally, it is important to stay motivated and keep your focus on your learning goals. Surround yourself with positive influences, such as books, podcasts, or people who inspire and encourage you, and remind yourself of the benefits of learning and the reasons why it is important to you.

Conclusion

Learning is a valuable and ongoing process that can bring many benefits to your life. By setting clear goals, creating a learning plan, and making learning a priority, you can maximize the impact of your efforts and reap the rewards of this important activity. Whether you are looking to improve your career prospects, expand your knowledge, or simply stay curious and engaged, ongoing learning is essential to your success and fulfillment.

24: The Benefits of Travel: Exploring the World and Discovering New Perspectives

Travel has a unique way of broadening our horizons and enriching our lives in ways we never thought possible. It exposes us to new cultures, different ways of living, and unique perspectives that can be life-changing. Whether it's a weekend getaway or a long-term trip, traveling has the power to inspire, motivate and rejuvenate our spirits, and can play a significant role in achieving lasting motivation.

One of the most obvious benefits of travel is that it allows us to experience new cultures and ways of life. This exposure to different lifestyles can broaden our minds and challenge our assumptions about the world. When we travel, we are forced to step outside of our comfort zone and confront new and sometimes uncomfortable situations. This experience can be life-changing and help us gain a greater appreciation and understanding of the world and its diverse cultures.

Travel can also be a source of inspiration. When we visit new places and experience new things, we often return home with a renewed sense of excitement and a fresh perspective on life. This can be a powerful motivator and can help us pursue our goals and dreams with renewed energy and determination. Whether it's trying new foods, visiting historic sites, or simply soaking in the beauty of a new place, travel can provide us with a wealth of inspiration to draw from.

In addition to being a source of inspiration, travel can also help boost our physical and mental health. Research has shown that travel can help reduce stress and improve our overall well-being. Traveling can also provide us with new experiences that can challenge us both mentally and physically, which can help us grow and develop as individuals.

One of the most important benefits of travel is that it can help us build strong relationships. When we travel with friends or family, we have the opportunity to bond and create memories that will last a lifetime. This shared experience can bring us closer together and strengthen our relationships, making us feel more connected and supported.

Travel can also provide us with a sense of adventure and excitement. Whether it's hiking a new trail, trying a new activity, or simply exploring a new place, travel allows us to push our boundaries and experience life in a new and exciting way. This sense of adventure can be a powerful motivator and can help us feel more alive and engaged in life.

In conclusion, travel is a powerful tool that can help us achieve lasting motivation. By exposing us to new cultures, providing us with a wealth of inspiration, improving our physical and mental health, building strong relationships, and providing us with a sense of adventure, travel can play a significant role in helping us achieve our goals and live a fulfilling life. So whether you're planning a trip to a nearby city or a journey to a far-off land, remember that travel can help unleash your inner drive and provide you with the ultimate guide to lasting motivation.

25: Building a Support System: Surrounding Yourself with Positive People

Building a support system is crucial for maintaining lasting motivation and achieving your goals. Surrounding yourself with positive and supportive people can provide you with the encouragement, motivation, and accountability you need to succeed. In this chapter, we'll discuss the benefits of having a support system and how to build one.

The first benefit of having a support system is that it provides you with encouragement and motivation. When you're feeling down or facing a challenge, your support system can help lift you up and remind you of your capabilities. They can offer words of encouragement and support, which can give you the boost you need to keep going.

Another benefit of having a support system is accountability. When you have people who are invested in your success, you're more likely to follow through on your goals. They can hold you accountable and encourage you to stay on track, which can increase your chances of success.

Having a support system can also help reduce stress and

anxiety. When you have people you can turn to for support, you'll feel more confident in your ability to handle challenges and overcome obstacles. This can reduce stress and anxiety, which can help you stay motivated and focused on your goals.

So, how do you build a support system? Here are a few tips to get you started:

— Seek out like-minded individuals. Look for people who share similar interests, goals, and values. These people are more likely to be supportive and encouraging.

— Join groups or organizations. Joining groups or organizations related to your interests or goals can help you connect with others who have similar interests and goals.

— Reach out to friends and family. Your friends and family can provide you with support and encouragement. Consider reaching out to them and sharing your goals with them.

— Find a mentor. A mentor can offer guidance and support as you work towards your goals. Consider reaching out to someone who has experience in your field or someone you admire and ask if they would be willing to serve as your mentor.

– Join an online community. There are many online communities where you can connect with others who share similar interests and goals. These communities can provide you with support, encouragement, and resources to help you achieve your goals.

Having a support system is crucial for maintaining lasting motivation and achieving your goals. By surrounding yourself with positive and supportive people, you'll have the encouragement, motivation, and accountability you need to succeed. So, start building your support system today and watch your motivation soar!

26: The Power of Personal Growth: Improving Yourself and Your Life

Personal growth is a vital aspect of a fulfilling life, and it is an ongoing process that requires effort, dedication, and a strong desire to improve yourself and your circumstances. Whether it's developing new skills, learning from your experiences, or setting new goals and aspirations, personal growth is about taking control of your life and becoming the best version of yourself. In this chapter, we will explore the benefits of personal growth and how you can harness the power of personal development to unleash your inner drive and achieve your goals.

First and foremost, personal growth is a powerful motivator. When you are actively working to improve yourself and your life, you are investing in yourself, and this investment can help you feel more confident, empowered, and capable of achieving your goals. Personal growth can also help you feel more fulfilled and satisfied with your life, as you are constantly working towards becoming the best version of yourself and achieving your aspirations.

26: THE POWER OF PERSONAL GROWTH: IMPROVING YOURSELF AND YOUR LIFE

One of the key benefits of personal growth is the development of new skills and abilities. Whether you are learning a new language, taking a course in a new subject, or developing a new hobby, personal growth allows you to expand your knowledge and skillset, making you more versatile and confident in your personal and professional life. This can help you pursue new opportunities, overcome challenges, and achieve your goals more effectively.

Another important aspect of personal growth is self-reflection. By taking the time to reflect on your experiences, beliefs, and values, you can gain a deeper understanding of yourself and your life. This can help you identify areas of your life that need improvement, and set realistic and achievable goals to make positive changes. Self-reflection can also help you build self-awareness and increase your emotional intelligence, allowing you to navigate life's challenges with greater ease.

Personal growth also requires discipline and consistency. By setting goals and regularly working towards them, you are actively taking control of your life and your future. Whether it's setting aside time each day to read, write, or exercise, or making changes to your daily habits and routines, discipline and consistency are key components of personal growth and success.

In addition to the personal benefits of personal growth, it can also have a positive impact on your relationships and the world around you. By improving yourself and your life, you are setting a positive example for others and making a positive impact in the world. Personal growth can also help you build stronger relationships with the people in your life, as you are able to better understand and communicate with those around you.

In conclusion, personal growth is a vital aspect of a fulfilling life, and it is an ongoing process that requires effort, dedication, and a strong desire to improve yourself and your circumstances. Whether it's developing new skills, learning from your experiences, or setting new goals and aspirations, personal growth is about taking control of your life and becoming the best version of yourself. By embracing the power of personal growth, you can unleash your inner drive and achieve your goals, living a fulfilling and satisfying life.

27: The Importance of Taking Breaks: Recharging Your Batteries

In our fast-paced world, it can be easy to become caught up in the hustle and bustle of daily life, constantly working and striving to achieve our goals. While hard work and determination are important traits to possess, it is equally important to take breaks and allow yourself to recharge. In this chapter, we will explore the importance of taking breaks and how they can benefit your overall health and well-being, as well as help you stay motivated and achieve your goals.

First and foremost, taking breaks helps to reduce stress and prevent burnout. When we work non-stop, our bodies and minds become overwhelmed and exhausted, leading to feelings of stress and frustration. This can make it difficult to concentrate, reduce our ability to make good decisions, and negatively impact our physical health. Taking regular breaks, however, can help to prevent burnout by allowing us to step back from our work and engage in activities that bring us joy and relaxation.

27: THE IMPORTANCE OF TAKING BREAKS: RECHARGING YOUR BATTERIES

In addition to reducing stress and preventing burnout, taking breaks can also improve our overall well-being. When we take breaks, we have the opportunity to engage in physical activity, connect with others, and participate in hobbies and interests that we enjoy. These activities help to reduce stress, boost our mood, and increase our energy levels, making us feel more refreshed and ready to tackle whatever challenges come our way.

Taking breaks also helps to improve our cognitive functioning, allowing us to work more effectively and efficiently when we return to our tasks. When we take a break, our minds are able to process information and form new connections, helping us to better understand and retain what we have learned. This, in turn, makes it easier for us to solve problems and make informed decisions.

Finally, taking breaks is essential for maintaining motivation and achieving our goals. When we work non-stop, it is easy to become demotivated and lose sight of our goals. Taking regular breaks, however, gives us the opportunity to reflect on our progress, celebrate our accomplishments, and refocus on what we want to achieve. This helps to keep us motivated and on track, and ensures that we continue to make progress towards our goals.

In conclusion, taking breaks is essential for maintaining our physical and mental health, improving our cognitive functioning, and achieving our goals. By allowing ourselves to step back from our work and engage in activities that bring us joy and relaxation, we can reduce stress, boost our mood, and improve our overall well-being. So, the next time you feel overwhelmed, take a break, recharge your batteries, and get back to work with renewed energy and motivation.

28: The Benefits of Volunteering: Making a Difference and Fulfilling Your Purpose

Volunteering is a powerful way to give back to your community, make a difference in the world, and fulfill your purpose. It provides numerous benefits to both the volunteer and the recipient of the volunteer's time and efforts. By taking the time to volunteer, you can help others, build relationships, and enrich your own life in the process.

One of the primary benefits of volunteering is the opportunity to give back to others and make a difference in the world. Whether you're volunteering at a local food bank, helping to build a house for a family in need, or participating in a fundraising event, you're making a positive impact on the lives of those around you. You're also helping to create a better, more compassionate world for everyone.

Another important benefit of volunteering is the opportunity to build relationships and connect with others. When you volunteer, you have the chance to meet new people and make new friends who share your passions and interests. You may even have the chance to work alongside someone who becomes a lifelong friend or mentor. The connections you make through volunteering can be incredibly meaningful and enriching, and can provide a sense of community and belonging that is often lacking in our busy, fast-paced lives.

In addition to the social benefits of volunteering, volunteering can also be incredibly fulfilling from a personal perspective. It provides an opportunity to use your skills and abilities to make a difference in the world and help others. Whether you're volunteering as a teacher, coach, mentor, or simply lending a helping hand, you're contributing to the greater good and making a difference in the lives of others. This sense of purpose and fulfillment can be incredibly motivating and can help you to find greater meaning and joy in your life.

Volunteering can also be a great way to boost your personal and professional skills. By volunteering in areas outside of your normal routine, you can gain new perspectives and broaden your horizons. You may also have the chance to develop new skills, such as leadership, communication, or problem-solving, which can be incredibly valuable in both your personal and professional life.

Finally, volunteering is a great way to take a break from the demands and pressures of everyday life. It provides an opportunity to escape the daily grind and focus on something that is truly meaningful and fulfilling. Whether you're volunteering once a week or once a year, the act of giving your time and energy to others can be incredibly energizing and rejuvenating. It can help you to recharge your batteries, feel more connected and fulfilled, and ultimately become more motivated and driven to achieve your goals.

In conclusion, volunteering is a powerful way to make a difference in the world, build relationships, and enrich your life. Whether you're volunteering to help others, develop new skills, or simply escape the demands of everyday life, volunteering is a valuable and rewarding experience. So why not get started today and unleash the power of volunteering in your life!

29: The Power of Positive Attitude: Embracing a Sunny Outlook on Life

"Attitude is a little thing that makes a big difference." - Winston Churchill

When it comes to motivation and success, having a positive attitude can make all the difference in the world. A positive attitude is a powerful force that can help you overcome obstacles, achieve your goals, and lead a fulfilling life. This chapter will explore the power of positive attitude and how you can cultivate one in your own life.

First, let's define what we mean by positive attitude. A positive attitude is a way of looking at life that is characterized by optimism, gratitude, and hope. It's a mindset that focuses on the good, the opportunities, and the possibilities rather than the challenges, the difficulties, and the negatives. A positive attitude can help you stay motivated and energized, even when faced with setbacks and obstacles.

One of the benefits of having a positive attitude is that it can help you stay motivated. When you have a positive outlook on life, you're more likely to see challenges as opportunities for growth and learning. This, in turn, can help you stay motivated and focused on your goals, even when faced with difficulties. For example, instead of seeing a challenging project as a burden, you might see it as an opportunity to learn and grow.

Another benefit of having a positive attitude is that it can help you build stronger relationships with others. People are naturally attracted to positive individuals, and when you have a positive attitude, you're more likely to make a positive impression on others. This can help you build stronger connections with others, which can be crucial in achieving your goals and leading a fulfilling life.

Positive attitude can also help you manage stress and lead to better health. When you have a positive outlook on life, you're less likely to feel overwhelmed by stress and more likely to cope effectively with challenges. This can have a positive impact on your physical and mental health, and can help you lead a more fulfilling life.

So, how can you cultivate a positive attitude in your own life? Here are some tips to get you started:

29: THE POWER OF POSITIVE ATTITUDE: EMBRACING A SUNNY OUTLOOK ON LIFE

– Practice gratitude: Start each day by focusing on the things you're grateful for. This can help you start your day on a positive note and set the tone for the rest of the day.

– Surround yourself with positive people: Seek out people who are positive and supportive, and limit your time with individuals who are negative or bring you down.

– Focus on the good: Make an effort to focus on the good things in your life, even when faced with challenges and difficulties.

– Practice mindfulness: Mindfulness is a great way to stay present and focused on the present moment. When you're mindful, you're less likely to be caught up in worries about the past or concerns about the future, and more likely to appreciate the present moment.

– Engage in activities that bring you joy: Make time for activities that bring you joy and fulfillment, and make them a regular part of your life.

– Cultivate a growth mindset: Focus on growth and learning, and see challenges as opportunities for growth and improvement.

– Surround yourself with positive affirmations: Surround yourself with positive affirmations, such as quotes, posters, or affirmations cards, to help keep you motivated and focused on your goals.

In conclusion, having a positive attitude can have a profound impact on your life. By embracing a sunny outlook, you can stay motivated, build stronger relationships, manage stress, and lead a fulfilling life. So, start today by focusing on the things you're grateful for, surrounding yourself with positive people

30: The Benefits of Creativity: Unleashing Your Imagination and Finding Your Voice

Creativity is an important aspect of our lives that often gets overlooked. It is more than just a hobby or a form of entertainment. Creativity can help us express ourselves in new and meaningful ways, connect with others, and provide a sense of purpose. In this chapter, we will explore the many benefits of creativity and why it is an essential component of a fulfilling life.

– Unleashing Your Imagination

One of the most significant benefits of creativity is that it allows us to unleash our imagination. Our minds are capable of generating limitless ideas and possibilities, and creativity is the key to unlocking this potential. When we engage in creative activities such as writing, painting, or music, we can let our imaginations run wild and tap into the vast well of our unconscious thoughts and emotions. This can help us better understand ourselves and our place in the world.

– Finding Your Voice

Creativity can also help us find our voice and express ourselves in new and meaningful ways. Many people struggle to articulate their thoughts and feelings, but through creative pursuits, they can find a means of expression that resonates with them. Whether it's through writing, art, or music, creativity provides a way for us to communicate our innermost thoughts and emotions in a way that is authentic and true to who we are.

– Connecting with Others

Creativity can also be a powerful tool for connecting with others. When we share our creative work with others, we open ourselves up to feedback, constructive criticism, and collaboration. This can help us build stronger relationships with others and foster a sense of community. Additionally, creative pursuits often bring people together, providing a platform for sharing and exploring common interests.

– Improving Mental Health

Creativity can have a positive impact on our mental health and well-being. Engaging in creative activities has been shown to reduce stress, anxiety, and depression, while also promoting feelings of happiness and well-being. This is because creativity provides a sense of flow, where we become fully absorbed in the activity and lose track of time. This flow state is characterized by feelings of joy and satisfaction, and can have a profound impact on our mental health.

– Boosting Confidence and Self-Esteem

Creativity can also play an important role in boosting our confidence and self-esteem. When we engage in creative activities, we take risks, push boundaries, and try new things. This can help us develop a sense of pride in our work, which in turn can help us feel more confident and self-assured. Furthermore, when others appreciate our creative work, it can provide validation and recognition, further boosting our self-esteem.

– Providing a Sense of Purpose

Finally, creativity can provide us with a sense of purpose and meaning in life. When we engage in creative activities, we can immerse ourselves in a world of our own creation, where the possibilities are limitless. This can help us find meaning in our lives and provides a sense of direction, guiding us towards our goals and aspirations.

In conclusion, creativity is an essential component of a fulfilling life. By unleashing our imaginations, finding our voices, connecting with others, improving our mental health, boosting our confidence and self-esteem, and providing a sense of purpose, creativity offers a wealth of benefits that cannot be found in any other aspect of our lives. So, whether you're an artist, a writer, a musician, or simply someone who loves to dabble in creative pursuits, embrace your creativity and let it be an integral part of your life.

31: Building a Fulfilling Career: Finding Work That Matters

Are you tired of feeling unfulfilled and uninspired by your work? Do you long to find a career that truly aligns with your values, passions, and purpose? If so, it's time to take action and build a fulfilling career.

A fulfilling career is one that allows you to use your strengths, pursue your interests, and make a positive impact on the world. It's a career that not only provides financial stability but also brings a sense of purpose, meaning, and satisfaction to your life.

Finding such a career requires effort, self-reflection, and a willingness to take risks. But the rewards are well worth it. When you find work that matters, you experience a sense of joy, energy, and motivation that you never thought possible.

Here are some tips to help you build a fulfilling career:

– Assess your values and passions. To find a career that truly aligns with your values and passions, you need to know what they are. Take some time to reflect on what is most important to you and what activities bring you the most joy and satisfaction. This will help you identify the types of careers that align with your values and interests.

– Consider your skills and strengths. In addition to your values and passions, it's also important to consider your skills and strengths. Think about what you excel at and what activities come naturally to you. Then, look for careers that allow you to use these skills and strengths.

– Network and explore. Once you have a clear idea of what you're looking for, start exploring your options. Talk to people in the industries that interest you, attend events, and read books and articles about different careers. This will give you a better understanding of what each career entails and whether it would be a good fit for you.

– Get practical experience. To truly understand what a career is like, it's important to gain practical experience. This could mean volunteering, taking on a part-time job, or completing an internship in the field you're interested in. This will give you a taste of what it would be like to work in that career and help you determine whether it's a good fit for you.

31: BUILDING A FULFILLING CAREER: FINDING WORK THAT MATTERS

– Be willing to take risks. Finding a fulfilling career often requires taking risks. This could mean leaving a secure job to pursue your passion, starting your own business, or taking a pay cut to work in a field that aligns with your values. While taking risks can be scary, it's important to remember that they are often necessary to find the career that truly fulfills you.

– Continuously grow and develop. Building a fulfilling career is not a one-time event, it's a journey. You need to continuously grow and develop your skills, explore new opportunities, and be open to change. This will help you stay motivated, engaged, and inspired by your work.

In conclusion, building a fulfilling career is a lifelong journey that requires effort, self-reflection, and a willingness to take risks. But when you find work that aligns with your values, passions, and purpose, the rewards are immeasurable. So take the time to assess your values and passions, explore your options, and be open to new opportunities. With persistence and determination, you can build a fulfilling career that will bring you joy, satisfaction, and motivation for years to come.

32: The Importance of Financial Health: Achieving Financial Freedom

Financial freedom is a term that refers to the state of having enough money to live comfortably without worrying about money. It is a goal that many people strive for, and it can provide a sense of security and peace of mind. However, achieving financial freedom is not always easy, and it often requires careful planning, smart decision-making, and discipline.

One of the keys to financial freedom is developing good money habits. This means living within your means, avoiding debt, and saving and investing regularly. It also means having a budget and tracking your spending so that you can see exactly where your money is going each month. This can help you make adjustments and cut back on expenses in order to reach your financial goals.

Another important aspect of financial health is having a diverse portfolio of investments. This can help you weather market fluctuations and reduce your overall risk. Some popular forms of investments include stocks, bonds, mutual funds, and real estate. It is important to do your research and seek the advice of a financial advisor when making investment decisions, as the wrong investments can lead to significant financial losses.

Having a healthy relationship with money is also crucial for financial freedom. This means learning to overcome any negative attitudes or beliefs you may have about money, and developing a positive relationship with it. This can involve learning about personal finance, setting financial goals, and focusing on your values and priorities.

Finally, having a plan for your financial future is essential. This means setting long-term financial goals and developing a strategy to achieve them. It may also involve seeking the advice of a financial advisor or professional who can help you create a personalized financial plan.

In conclusion, financial health is a crucial component of a fulfilling life, and it is never too late to start working towards financial freedom. By developing good money habits, investing wisely, having a positive attitude towards money, and planning for your financial future, you can achieve financial freedom and live a life without financial worries.

33: The Benefits of Giving Back: Making a Difference in Your Community

Giving back to your community is a powerful way to make a difference in the world and to fulfill your purpose. By volunteering your time and resources, you can improve the lives of others and build a sense of fulfillment and purpose. In this chapter, we will explore the many benefits of giving back and how it can help you to unleash your inner drive and achieve your goals.

First and foremost, giving back to your community is a great way to feel good about yourself. When you volunteer your time and resources, you can see the positive impact that you are making on others. This sense of fulfillment and purpose is essential for lasting motivation, as it gives you a clear reason to continue striving towards your goals.

In addition to providing a sense of fulfillment, giving back to your community can also help you to build stronger relationships. By working together with others towards a common goal, you can develop a sense of community and camaraderie. This can help you to feel more connected to others, and to build stronger relationships with the people in your life.

Another benefit of giving back to your community is that it can help you to develop new skills and to expand your horizons. When you volunteer, you are often asked to perform tasks that are outside of your comfort zone. By doing so, you can learn new skills and gain experience in areas that you may not have had the opportunity to explore otherwise. This can be a great way to grow as a person and to expand your horizons.

Finally, giving back to your community can be a powerful way to help you to achieve your goals. When you volunteer, you are often working towards a common goal with others. This shared effort can help you to stay motivated and focused, as you work towards a common objective. In addition, giving back to your community can also help you to develop a strong sense of purpose and direction, which is essential for achieving your goals.

In conclusion, the benefits of giving back to your community are numerous and far-reaching. Whether you are looking to improve the lives of others, build stronger relationships, develop new skills, or achieve your goals, giving back is a powerful way to unleash your inner drive and achieve your purpose. So why not start today, and find ways to make a difference in your community?

34: Building a Fulfilling Life: Finding Happiness and Fulfillment

Life is a journey, and everyone's journey is different. Some people are driven by a desire for success, while others are motivated by the pursuit of happiness. But no matter what your individual goals and desires may be, one thing is certain: in order to truly live a fulfilling life, you need to be motivated and engaged. This chapter will explore the importance of finding happiness and fulfillment in life, and will offer tips and strategies for building a life that truly satisfies and inspires you.

The first step in building a fulfilling life is to understand what happiness and fulfillment actually mean to you. For some people, happiness might be defined by material wealth and success, while for others, it might be found in the simple pleasures of daily life. There is no right or wrong answer when it comes to what happiness and fulfillment mean, as long as they align with your personal values and priorities.

Once you have a clear understanding of what happiness and

fulfillment mean to you, you can start to create a plan for building a life that is truly fulfilling. This might involve setting new goals, exploring new interests and hobbies, and reaching out to new people and communities. It might also involve letting go of negative thoughts and habits that are holding you back, and embracing positive, empowering thoughts and behaviors that support your happiness and well-being.

One key aspect of building a fulfilling life is to prioritize your own needs and desires. This means taking care of yourself both physically and emotionally, and making time for self-care and relaxation. This might involve exercise, meditation, or simply taking a long, hot bath. Whatever makes you feel happy and relaxed, be sure to make time for it in your life.

Another important aspect of building a fulfilling life is to cultivate positive relationships with others. Whether it's spending time with family and friends, or volunteering in your community, connecting with others in meaningful ways can bring a great deal of joy and fulfillment to your life. It's also important to surround yourself with people who support and encourage you, and to let go of relationships that are toxic or draining.

Finally, it's important to embrace a spirit of generosity and compassion, both in your own life and in the lives of those around you. Whether it's through volunteering, donating money, or simply offering a listening ear to someone who needs it, giving back to others can help you feel more connected and fulfilled, and can make a difference in the world.

In conclusion, building a fulfilling life is a journey that requires effort and dedication, but it is a journey that is well worth taking. By understanding what happiness and fulfillment mean to you, prioritizing your own needs and desires, cultivating positive relationships, and embracing a spirit of generosity and compassion, you can create a life that is truly inspiring and satisfying. So take the first step today, and start building the life you deserve.

35: The Power of Legacy: Leaving Your Mark on the World

Legacy. It's a word that often evokes thoughts of wealth, fame, and power. But the truth is, legacy is something much more personal and meaningful. It's about the impact you make on the world, the memories you leave behind, and the influence you have on future generations. Building a legacy is not just about achieving greatness, it's about making a difference in the world and inspiring others to do the same.

In today's fast-paced world, it's easy to get caught up in the pursuit of success and forget about what truly matters. We often get so caught up in our own lives that we forget to make a positive impact on the world around us. However, by focusing on our legacy, we can shift our focus from personal success to something much more meaningful and enduring.

One of the most powerful ways to build a legacy is through giving back. Whether it's through volunteer work, supporting a cause you believe in, or simply being kind to others, the act of giving back can have a profound impact on your life and the lives of others. When you make a positive difference in someone else's life, you are creating a ripple effect that will continue to spread for years to come.

In addition to giving back, building a fulfilling life is also an important part of creating a legacy. By pursuing your passions and finding happiness and fulfillment, you inspire others to do the same. Your life becomes a testament to what is possible and serves as a source of inspiration for future generations.

Finally, by leaving a lasting impact on the world, you create a legacy that will continue to inspire and influence others long after you're gone. Whether it's through your work, your relationships, or your community, your legacy is a way of making a difference in the world and leaving a mark on future generations.

So, what is your legacy? What impact do you want to have on the world? The answer to these questions may not come to you immediately, but by focusing on your legacy, you can create a life that is truly meaningful and fulfilling. Whether it's through giving back, building a fulfilling life, or leaving a lasting impact, the ultimate goal is to make a difference in the world and inspire others to do the same.

35: THE POWER OF LEGACY: LEAVING YOUR MARK ON THE WORLD

In conclusion, the power of legacy is something that should not be underestimated. By focusing on your legacy, you can shift your focus from personal success to something much more meaningful and enduring. So, take a moment to reflect on your life and think about the impact you want to have on the world. Your legacy is waiting for you to create it, and the possibilities are truly endless.

36: The Ultimate Guide to Lasting Motivation: Your Blueprint for a Fulfilling Life

In the final chapter of this guide to motivation, we will explore the ultimate blueprint for a fulfilling life. This blueprint incorporates all of the strategies, techniques, and philosophies outlined in the previous chapters, and serves as a roadmap for how you can achieve your goals, fulfill your potential, and live a happy and satisfying life.

The first step in creating your blueprint is to identify your values, beliefs, and priorities. What is important to you? What do you believe in? What do you want to accomplish in life? These are the questions you need to ask yourself in order to determine your core values and guiding principles.

Next, you need to set clear, achievable goals for yourself. This means defining what you want to accomplish in various areas of your life, such as your career, relationships, health, personal growth, and finances. Be sure to set both short-term and long-term goals, and make sure they are specific, measurable, and time-bound.

Once you have your goals in place, it is time to take action.

This means developing a plan of action that will help you achieve your goals and make progress towards your ultimate vision for your life. This may involve seeking out new opportunities, learning new skills, seeking out mentorship or guidance, or making changes in your daily habits and routines.

Another important aspect of your blueprint is building a support system. Surrounding yourself with positive, supportive people who share your values and goals is crucial for staying motivated and on track. This may mean seeking out friends, family members, or professional mentors who can help you stay motivated and provide you with the support you need.

In addition to taking action and building a support system, it is also important to maintain a positive attitude and cultivate a sense of gratitude. This means focusing on the good things in your life, embracing challenges and setbacks as opportunities for growth, and keeping a sense of perspective when things don't go as planned.

Finally, it is important to make time for self-care and to recharge your batteries. This may involve taking breaks, practicing mindfulness and meditation, engaging in hobbies and interests, or simply taking time to relax and recharge.

By following this ultimate blueprint for a fulfilling life, you can unleash your inner drive, achieve your goals, and live a life that is filled with happiness, purpose, and meaning. Whether you are just starting out on your journey or looking to take your motivation to the next level, this guide will help you find lasting motivation and fulfill your potential.

Thank You

As we reach the end of this book, I want to say thanks for reading this book.

I want to get this information out to as many people as possible. If you found this book helpful, I would greatly appreciate you leaving me a review. This helps others find the book as well.

Disclaimer

This document is geared towards providing exact and reliable information in regards to the topic and issue covered. The publication is sold on the idea that the publisher is not required to render an accounting, officially permitted, or otherwise, qualified services. If advice is necessary, legal, financial, medical or professional, a practiced individual in the profession should be ordered.

This information is not presented by a financial or medical practitioner and is for entertainment, educational and informational purposes only. The content is not intended as a substitute for professional medical advice, diagnosis, or treatment. Always seek the advice of your physician or other qualified health care provider with any questions you may have regarding a medical condition. Never disregard professional medical advice or delay in seeking it because of something you have read.

The information provided herein is stated to be truthful and consistent, in that any liability, in terms of inattention or otherwise, by any usage or abuse of any policies, processes, or directions contained within is the solitary and utter responsibility of the recipient reader. Under no circumstances

DISCLAIMER

will any legal responsibility or blame be held against the publisher for any reparation, damages, or monetary loss due to the information herein, either directly or indirectly.